1 & 2
THESSALONIANS

Hope for a Better Tomorrow

LOVEGODGREATLY.COM

1 & 2 THESSALONIANS: HOPE FOR A BETTER TOMORROW

Copyright © 2018 by Love God Greatly Ministry

Permission is granted to print and reproduce this document for the purpose of completing the *1 & 2 Thessalonians: Hope for a Better Tomorrow* online Bible study. Please do not alter this document in any way. All rights reserved.

Published in Dallas by Love God Greatly.

Special thanks to:
Meshali Mitchell - Various photos

Unless otherwise noted, Scripture quotations are taken from *The Holy Bible, English Standard Version* Copyright © 2001 by Crossway Bibles, a publishing ministry of Good News Publishers.

Printed in the United States of America

Library of Congress Cataloging-in-Publication Data

Printed in the United States of America

23   22   21   20   19   18

6   5   4   3   2   1

AT LOVE GOD GREATLY, YOU'LL FIND
REAL, AUTHENTIC WOMEN. WOMEN WHO
ARE IMPERFECT, YET FORGIVEN.

Women who desire less of us, and a whole lot
more of Jesus. Women who long to know God
through His Word, because we know that Truth
transforms and sets us free. Women who are
better together, saturated in God's Word and in
community with one another.

Welcome, friend. We're so glad you're here...

CONTENTS

WELCOME

We are glad you have decided to join us in this Bible study! First of all, please know that you have been prayed for! It is not a coincidence you are participating in this study.

Our prayer for you is simple: that you will grow closer to our Lord as you dig into His Word each and every day! As you develop the discipline of being in God's Word on a daily basis, our prayer is that you will fall in love with Him even more as you spend time reading from the Bible.

Each day before you read the assigned Scripture(s), pray and ask God to help you understand it. Invite Him to speak to you through His Word. Then listen. It's His job to speak to you, and it's your job to listen and obey.

Take time to read the verses over and over again. We are told in Proverbs to search and you will find: "Search for it like silver, and hunt for it like hidden treasure. Then you will understand" (Prov. 2:4–5 NCV).

All of us here at Love God Greatly can't wait for you to get started, and we hope to see you at the finish line. Endure, persevere, press on—and don't give up! Finish well what you are beginning today. We will be here every step of the way, cheering you on! We are in this together. Fight to rise early, to push back the stress of the day, to sit alone and spend time in God's Word! Let's see what God has in store for you in this study! Journey with us as we learn to love God greatly with our lives!

As you go through this study, join us in the following resources below:

Weekly Blog Posts •

Weekly Memory Verses •

Weekly Challenges •

Facebook, Twitter, Instagram •

LoveGodGreatly.com •

Hashtags: #LoveGodGreatly •

RESOURCES

Join Us

ONLINE
lovegodgreatly.com

STORE
lovegodgreatly.com/store

FACEBOOK
facebook.com/LoveGodGreatly

INSTAGRAM
instagram.com/lovegodgreatlyofficial

TWITTER
@_LoveGodGreatly

DOWNLOAD THE APP

CONTACT US
info@lovegodgreatly.com

CONNECT
#LoveGodGreatly

LOVE
GOD
GREATLY

Love God Greatly (LGG) is a beautiful community of women who use a variety of technology platforms to keep each other accountable in God's Word. We start with a simple Bible reading plan, but it doesn't stop there.

Some women gather in homes and churches locally, while others connect online with women across the globe. Whatever the method, we lovingly lock arms and unite for this purpose: to love God greatly with our lives.

In today's fast-paced technology-driven world, it would be easy to study God's Word in an isolated environment that lacks encouragement or support, but that isn't the intention here at Love God Greatly. God created us to live in community with Him and with those around us.

Would you consider reaching out and doing this study with someone?

We need each other, and we live life better together. Because of this, would you consider reaching out and doing this study with someone?

Rest assured we'll be studying right alongside you—learning with you, cheering for you, enjoying sweet fellowship, and smiling from ear to ear as we watch God unite women together—intentionally connecting hearts and minds for His glory.

So here's the challenge: call your mom, your sister, your grandma, the girl across the street, or the college friend across the country. Gather a group of girls from your church or workplace, or meet in a coffee shop with friends you have always wished you knew better.

Arm-in-arm and hand-in-hand, let's do this thing…together.

SOAP STUDY
HOW AND WHY TO SOAP

In this study we offer you a study journal to accompany the verses we are reading. This journal is designed to help you interact with God's Word and learn to dig deeper, encouraging you to slow down and reflect on what God is saying to you that day.

At Love God Greatly, we use the SOAP Bible study method. Before beginning, let's take a moment to define this method and share why we recommend using it during your quiet time in the following pages.

The most important ingredients in the Soap method are your interaction with God's Word and your application of His Word to your life.

It's one thing to simply read Scripture. But when you interact with it, intentionally slowing down to really reflect on it, suddenly words start popping off the page. The SOAP method allows you to dig deeper into Scripture and see more than you would if you simply read the verses and then went on your merry way.

The most important ingredients in the SOAP method are your interaction with God's Word and your application of His Word to your life:

Blessed is the one who does not walk in step with the wicked or stand in the way that sinners take or sit in the company of mockers, but whose delight is in the law of the LORD, and who meditates on his law day and night. That person is like a tree planted by streams of water, which yields its fruit in season and whose leaf does not wither—whatever they do prospers.
(Ps. 1:1–3, NIV)

Please take the time to SOAP through our Bible studies and see for yourself how much more you get from your daily reading.

You'll be amazed.

SOAP STUDY (CONTINUED)
WHAT DOES SOAP MEAN?

S STANDS FOR
SCRIPTURE

Physically write out the verses.

You'll be amazed at what God will reveal to you just by taking the time to slow down and write out what you are reading!

MONDAY

READ
Colossians 1:5–8

SOAP
Colossians 1:5–8

Scripture

WRITE
OUT THE
SCRIPTURE
PASSAGE
FOR THE
DAY.

The faith and love that spring from the hope stored up for you in heaven and about which you have already heard in the true message of the gospel that has come to you. In the same way the gospel is bearing fruit and growing throughout the whole world just as it has been doing among you since the day you heard it and truly understood God's grace. You learned it from Epaphras, our dear fellow servant, who is a faithful minister of Christ on our behalf, and who also told us of your love in the Spirit.

Observations

WRITE
DOWN 1 OR 2
OBSERVATIONS
FROM THE
PASSAGE

When you combine faith and love, you get hope. We must remember that our hope is in heaven; it is yet to come. The gospel is the Word of truth. This gospel is continually bearing fruit and growing from the first day to the last. It just takes one person to change a whole community. Epaphras.

O STANDS FOR
OBSERVATION

What do you see in the verses that you're reading?

Who is the intended audience? Is there a repetition of words?

What words stand out to you?

A STANDS FOR
APPLICATION

This is when God's Word becomes personal.

What is God saying to you today?

How can you apply what you just read to your own personal life?

What changes do you need to make? Is there action you need to take?

Applications

WRITE DOWN 1 OR 2 APPLICATIONS FROM THE PASSAGE.

God used one man, Epaphras, to change a whole town. I was reminded that we are simply called to tell others about Christ; it is God's job to spread the gospel, to grow it, and have it bear fruit. I felt today's verses were almost directly spoken to Love God Greatly women: The gospel is bearing fruit and growing throughout the whole world just as it has been doing among you since the day you heard it and truly understood God's grace.

Pray

WRITE OUT A PRAYER OVER WHAT YOU LEARNED FROM TODAY'S PASSAGE.

Dear Lord, please help me to be an Epaphras, to tell others about You and then leave the results in Your loving hands. Please help me to understand and apply personally what I have read today to my life, thereby becoming more and more like You each and every day. Help me to live a life that bears the fruit of faith and love, anchoring my hope in heaven, not here on earth. Help me to remember that the best is yet to come!

P STANDS FOR **PRAYER**

Pray God's Word back to Him. Spend time thanking Him.

If He has revealed something to you during this time in His Word, pray about it.

If He has revealed some sin that is in your life, confess. And remember, He loves you dearly.

A RECIPE FOR YOU

BANITSA - БАНИЦА

Traditional Bulgarian food, made by layering a mixture of eggs and cheese and filo dough. Traditionally Banitsa is made with homemade filo dough sheets, but store-bought filo is great here too! Banitsa is usually a breakfast food and can be served hot or cold with yogurt.

Serves 4-6 people.

Ingredients

12 Sheets Filo Dough, thawed

4 Eggs

1/2 lb. Bulgarian white cheese (Feta cheese is good substitute), crumbled

1 1/2 cups Plain Greek yogurt

8 tablespoons (1 stick) butter, melted

Salt

Directions

- Preheat oven to 350 F (180 C)
- Whisk eggs and mix with cheese, yogurt and salt in a bowl.
- Melt the butter.
- Take 3 sheets of filo and brush with butter. Take about 1/4 of the egg mixture and spread on top of buttered filo sheets.
- Roll the sheets, forming a long roll. Repeat 4 more times, so that at the end there are 4 long rolls of filo and filling.
- Take one of the rolls and place it in a round baking dish, along the edge. Keep placing the rolls in the dish, forming a spiral towards the center of the baking dish.
- Brush top of banitsa with the left over melted butter.
- Bake for about 40 minutes.
- Take the banitsa out of the oven. If you want it to be crunchy, let it cool down and enjoy! If you want it to be soft, cover the banitsa with a dish towel after you take it out and let cool. Enjoy!

HOMEMADE FILO DOUGH

Ingredients

4 Cups Flour

1 Teaspoon Salt

1 1/3 Cup Room Temperature Water

1/4 Cup Olive Oil

Directions

- Mix flour and salt in a mixing bowl.
- Add water and oil and mix until a soft dough is formed.
- Knead dough in the bowl for about 10 minutes. Dough will be sticky at first, but as you knead it will become smooth. Wrap the bowl with plastic wrap and let dough rest at room temperature for about an hour.
- Divide the dough into 12 balls. Take one dough ball and place on a floured surface. Roll it with a rolling pin.
- Repeat with the rest of the dough and use instead of the store-bought filo.

LGG BULGARIAN TESTIMONY

DENITZA, UNITED STATES

My name is Denitza. I'm one of the ladies that translates LGG materials in Bulgarian.

I started translating in May of 2017 and became a member of the Bulgarian Facebook group. The group was started by Krassy Hristova, who is the co-translator for the Bulgarian studies.

I have met amazing Christian women from my native country!

I live in the U.S.A. and accepted Christ as my Savior few years after I came to the country. Thanks to my husband, I know and follow the One and Only true God!

I had never read or seen a Bible in Bulgarian before I started translating. I was so unsure if I could translate the materials correctly. I started the studies in English in October of 2016 and knew how great the materials were. LGG has helped me to grow closer to God, while studying the Word with other Christian women. I wanted the same for the ladies in Bulgaria. God helped me to translate, so that women from my country can benefit from the study materials. In the process of translating and helping Krassy with the group, I have met amazing Christian women from my native country! They are filled with love for God and strong faith!

I pray our translations will reach many women, and give them encouragement and hope, just like I have received from Love God Greatly!

LGG BULGARIAN TESTIMONY

KRASSI, BULGARIA

Hello. My name is Krassi Hristova. I am 38-years-old, married and we have a little girl. I was born in a small town in south Bulgaria called Smolyan. I came to know Jesus through my grandparents.

Ten years ago, my family emigrated to Spain. I did not speak Spanish, so I did not attend a church. During a difficult moment, I was praying. One day, passing thru the town, I saw the building of an evangelical church. An answer to my prayers! A few days later I went back to pray with brothers and sisters in Christ.

At one regional assembly the speaker presented an Ama A Dios Grandemente- the Spanish section of LGG. They were studying the book of Ecclesiastes - I love this book! At home, I wanted to share it with a cousin of mine who lives in Bulgaria, and that is how I started to translate into Bulgarian. Later, God brought Danitza Neville here. Now we have a Facebook group and page "Обичай Бог Всеотдайно"- LGG Bulgaria.

I know that every one of us needs to have a special, intimate relationship with our God, and the LGG journals are just the perfect instrument to do establish it. Step by step, day by day, digging into Gods Word.

To connect with LGG Bulgarian Branch:

• facebook.com/lggbulgaria

Do you know someone who could use our *Love God Greatly* Bible studies in Bulgarian? If so, make sure and tell them about LGG Bulgarian and all the amazing Bible study resources we provide to help equip them with God's Word!!!

Every one of us needs to have a special, intimate relationship with our God.

1 & 2
THESSALONIANS

Hope for a Better Tomorrow

Let's Begin

INTRODUCTION

1 & 2 THESSALONIANS

Authenticity. It's one thing people are beginning to value more and more. We want real friends, with whom we can be transparent and who love us despite our shortcomings. We want to be able to talk about real concerns and not just have superficial conversations. We not only WANT authenticity, we NEED it.

But sometimes the Bible, where we go for truth, can seem a bit unreal. We read of men and women whom we consider "giants of the faith" and skim over their failures. We read of men who endure significant suffering with incredible steadfastness and hope, and we have trouble relating to them. But the more carefully we read we will see that the Bible does not shy away from showing us real struggles and the gritty aspects of the faith.

1st & 2nd Thessalonians are two great examples for us. In these letters, written by Paul, we read about Christians who were doing well in some areas, like loving each other, but struggling in others, like obsessing over the coming of Jesus and being lazy and idle.

In the book of Acts, we learn how the church in Thessalonica was formed. It all started with a vision in which a man said to Paul, "Come over into Macedonia and help us" (Acts 16:9). And so, Paul along with Silas, Luke and Timothy went, first to Philippi and then to Thessalonica, where they started a church in each city. This was Paul's second missionary journey.

Shortly after Paul started the church, opposition arose to such an extent that Paul was forced to leave. In fact, the danger was so great that Paul escaped in the middle of the night (Acts 17:1-10)! After Paul's sudden departure, this young church was exposed to persecution, and Paul became concerned about their faith and their well-being. So, he sent Timothy to the Thessalonian church to check on them and report back.

Timothy had good news to share with Paul! The Christians in Thessalonica were doing well. They were keeping the faith, clinging to the gospel, and loving each other. But, because all churches are made up of sinners, there were also some problems.

Some were concerned about what would happen to those who died before Christ came back, some were neglecting to work out their personal faith, and others were dealing with ethical issues. So Paul wrote to them, addressing these problems and reassuring them of his love.

In 2nd Thessalonians Paul addresses more deeply some of the misconceptions the church had regarding Christ's second coming. There were some who believed that Jesus was going to return very shortly, therefore they didn't need to work, and so idleness became a real problem. Paul gets serious, letting them (and us) know that it is inappropriate for followers of God to be lazy and mooch off of the goodness, hard work, and wealth of others.

As with all of Paul's books, his writings include robust, profound theology and practical application. Paul directly and plainly points out the errors of the believers but also points his audience to the grace and hope found in their Redeemer, Christ Jesus.

As you immerse yourself in the books of 1st & 2nd Thessalonians, ask yourself what you learn about the Gospel and how this should impact how you live your life today.

READING PLAN

ENTRUSTED WITH THE GOSPEL

Monday
Read: 1 Thessalonians 1:1-3
SOAP: 1 Thessalonians 1:2-3

Tuesday
Read: 1 Thessalonians 1:4-10
SOAP: 1 Thessalonians 1:4-5

Wednesday
Read: 1 Thessalonians 2:1-8
SOAP: 1 Thessalonians 2:8

Thursday
Read: 1 Thessalonians 2:9-16
SOAP: 1 Thessalonians 2:12-13

Friday
Read: 1 Thessalonians 2:17-20
SOAP: 1 Thessalonians 2:19-20

STANDING FIRM IN FAITH, HOPE & LOVE

Monday
Read: 1 Thessalonians 3:1-5
SOAP: 1 Thessalonians 3:2-3

Tuesday
Read: 1 Thessalonians 3:6-13
SOAP: 1 Thessalonians 3:11-13

Wednesday
Read: 1 Thessalonians 4:1-8
SOAP: 1 Thessalonians 4:3-5

Thursday
Read: 1 Thessalonians 4:9-12
SOAP: 1 Thessalonians 4:11-12

Friday
Read: 1 Thessalonians 4:13-18
SOAP: 1 Thessalonians 4:13-14

HOLD ON
TO THE GOOD

Monday
Read: 1 Thessalonians 5:1-3
SOAP: 1 Thessalonians 5:2

Tuesday
Read: 1 Thessalonians 5:4-8
SOAP: 1 Thessalonians 5:8

Wednesday
Read: 1 Thessalonians 5:9-11
SOAP: 1 Thessalonians 5:9-11

Thursday
Read: 1 Thessalonians 5:12-22
SOAP: 1 Thessalonians 5: 14-18

Friday
Read: 1 Thessalonians 5:23-28
SOAP: 1 Thessalonians 5:24

WEEK 4

THE HOPE OF
CHRIST'S RETURN

Monday
Read: 2 Thessalonians 1:1-2
SOAP: 2 Thessalonians 1:2

Tuesday
Read: 2 Thessalonians 1:3-4
SOAP: 2 Thessalonians 1:3-4

Wednesday
Read: 2 Thessalonians 1:5-8
SOAP: 2 Thessalonians 1:6-8

Thursday
Read: 2 Thessalonians 1:9-10
SOAP: 2 Thessalonians 1:10

Friday
Read: 2 Thessalonians 1:11-12
SOAP: 2 Thessalonians 1:11

OUR GOOD HOPE

Monday
Read: 2 Thessalonians 2:1-2
SOAP: 2 Thessalonians 2:2

Tuesday
Read: 2 Thessalonians 2:3-4
SOAP: 2 Thessalonians 2:3

Wednesday
Read: 2 Thessalonians 2:5-8
SOAP: 2 Thessalonians 2:7

Thursday
Read: 2 Thessalonians 2:9-12
SOAP: 2 Thessalonians 2:10

Friday
Read: 2 Thessalonians 2:13-17
SOAP: 2 Thessalonians 2:13

PRAYING
& WORKING

Monday
Read: 2 Thessalonians 3:1-5
SOAP: 2 Thessalonians 3:3

Tuesday
Read: 2 Thessalonians 3:6-9
SOAP: 2 Thessalonians 3:9

Wednesday
Read: 2 Thessalonians 3:10-12
SOAP: 2 Thessalonians 3:10

Thursday
Read: 2 Thessalonians 3:13-15
SOAP: 2 Thessalonians 3:13

Friday
Read: 2 Thessalonians 3:16-18
SOAP: 2 Thessalonians 3:16

YOUR GOALS

We believe it's important to write out goals for this study. Take some time now and write three goals you would like to focus on as you begin to rise each day and dig into God's Word. Make sure and refer back to these goals throughout the next weeks to help you stay focused. You can do it!

1.

2.

3.

Signature:

Date:

WEEK 1

Entrusted With The Gospel

We exhorted each one of you and encouraged you and charged you to walk in a manner worthy of God, who calls you into His own kingdom and glory.

1 THESSALONIANS. 2:12

PRAYER

WRITE DOWN YOUR PRAYER REQUESTS
AND PRAISES FOR EACH DAY.

Prayer focus for this week:
Spend time praying for your family members.

MONDAY

TUESDAY

WEDNESDAY

THURSDAY

FRIDAY

CHALLENGE

You can find this listed in our Monday blog post.

MONDAY
Scripture for Week 1

1 Thessalonians 1:1-3
1 Paul, Silvanus, and Timothy,

To the church of the Thessalonians in God the Father and the Lord Jesus Christ:

Grace to you and peace.

2 We give thanks to God always for all of you, constantly mentioning you in our prayers, 3 remembering before our God and Father your work of faith and labor of love and steadfastness of hope in our Lord Jesus Christ.

MONDAY

READ:
1 Thessalonians 1:1-3

SOAP:
1 Thessalonians 1:2-3

Scripture

WRITE
OUT THE
SCRIPTURE
PASSAGE
FOR THE
DAY.

Observations

WRITE
DOWN 1 OR 2
OBSERVATIONS
FROM THE
PASSAGE.

Applications

WRITE
DOWN 1 OR 2
APPLICATIONS
FROM THE
PASSAGE.

Pray

WRITE OUT
A PRAYER
OVER WHAT
YOU LEARNED
FROM TODAY'S
PASSAGE.

TUESDAY
Scripture for Week 1

1 Thessalonians 1:4-10
4 For we know, brothers loved by God, that he has chosen
you, 5 because our gospel came to you not only in word, but also
in power and in the Holy Spirit and with full conviction. You
know what kind of men we proved to be among you for your
sake. 6 And you became imitators of us and of the Lord, for you
received the word in much affliction, with the joy of the Holy
Spirit, 7 so that you became an example to all the believers in
Macedonia and in Achaia. 8 For not only has the word of the
Lord sounded forth from you in Macedonia and Achaia, but your
faith in God has gone forth everywhere, so that we need not say
anything. 9 For they themselves report concerning us the kind
of reception we had among you, and how you turned to God from
idols to serve the living and true God, 10 and to wait for his
Son from heaven, whom he raised from the dead, Jesus who delivers
us from the wrath to come.

TUESDAY

READ:
1 Thessalonians 1:4-10

SOAP:
1 Thessalonians 1:4-5

Scripture

WRITE
OUT THE
SCRIPTURE
PASSAGE
FOR THE
DAY.

Observations

WRITE
DOWN 1 OR 2
OBSERVATIONS
FROM THE
PASSAGE.

Applications

WRITE
DOWN 1 OR 2
APPLICATIONS
FROM THE
PASSAGE.

Pray

WRITE OUT
A PRAYER
OVER WHAT
YOU LEARNED
FROM TODAY'S
PASSAGE.

WEDNESDAY
Scripture for Week 1

1 Thessalonians 2:1-8

1 For you yourselves know, brothers, that our coming to you was not in vain.2 But though we had already suffered and been shamefully treated at Philippi, as you know, we had boldness in our God to declare to you the gospel of God in the midst of much conflict. 3 For our appeal does not spring from error or impurity or any attempt to deceive, 4 but just as we have been approved by God to be entrusted with the gospel, so we speak, not to please man, but to please God who tests our hearts. 5 For we never came with words of flattery, as you know, nor with a pretext for greed—God is witness. 6 Nor did we seek glory from people, whether from you or from others, though we could have made demands as apostles of Christ. 7 But we were gentle among you, like a nursing mother taking care of her own children. 8 So, being affectionately desirous of you, we were ready to share with you not only the gospel of God but also our own selves, because you had become very dear to us.

WEDNESDAY

READ:
1 Thessalonians 2:1-8

SOAP:
1 Thessalonians 2:8

Scripture

WRITE
OUT THE
SCRIPTURE
PASSAGE
FOR THE
DAY.

Observations

WRITE
DOWN 1 OR 2
OBSERVATIONS
FROM THE
PASSAGE.

Applications

WRITE
DOWN 1 OR 2
APPLICATIONS
FROM THE
PASSAGE.

Pray

WRITE OUT
A PRAYER
OVER WHAT
YOU LEARNED
FROM TODAY'S
PASSAGE.

THURSDAY
Scripture for Week 1

1 Thessalonians 2:9-16

9 For you remember, brothers, our labor and toil: we worked
night and day, that we might not be a burden to any of you, while
we proclaimed to you the gospel of God. 10 You are witnesses,
and God also, how holy and righteous and blameless was our
conduct toward you believers. 11 For you know how, like a father
with his children, 12 we exhorted each one of you and encouraged
you and charged you to walk in a manner worthy of God, who calls
you into his own kingdom and glory.

13 And we also thank God constantly for this, that when
you received the word of God, which you heard from us, you
accepted it not as the word of men but as what it really is, the
word of God, which is at work in you believers. 14 For you,
brothers, became imitators of the churches of God in Christ Jesus
that are in Judea. For you suffered the same things from your
own countrymen as they did from the Jews, 15 who killed both
the Lord Jesus and the prophets, and drove us out, and displease
God and oppose all mankind 16 by hindering us from speaking to
the Gentiles that they might be saved—so as always to fill up the
measure of their sins. But wrath has come upon them at last!

THURSDAY

READ:
1 Thessalonians 2:9-16

SOAP:
1 Thessalonians 2:12-13

Scripture

WRITE
OUT THE
SCRIPTURE
PASSAGE
FOR THE
DAY.

Observations

WRITE
DOWN 1 OR 2
OBSERVATIONS
FROM THE
PASSAGE.

Applications

WRITE
DOWN 1 OR 2
APPLICATIONS
FROM THE
PASSAGE.

Pray

WRITE OUT
A PRAYER
OVER WHAT
YOU LEARNED
FROM TODAY'S
PASSAGE.

FRIDAY
Scripture for Week 1

1 Thessalonians 2:17-20

17 But since we were torn away from you, brothers, for a short time, in person not in heart, we endeavored the more eagerly and with great desire to see you face to face, 18 because we wanted to come to you—I, Paul, again and again—but Satan hindered us. 19 For what is our hope or joy or crown of boasting before our Lord Jesus at his coming? Is it not you? 20 For you are our glory and joy.

FRIDAY

READ:
1 Thessalonians 2:17-20

SOAP:
1 Thessalonians 2:19-20

Scripture

WRITE
OUT THE
SCRIPTURE
PASSAGE
FOR THE
DAY.

Observations

WRITE
DOWN 1 OR 2
OBSERVATIONS
FROM THE
PASSAGE.

Applications

WRITE
DOWN 1 OR 2
APPLICATIONS
FROM THE
PASSAGE.

Pray

WRITE OUT
A PRAYER
OVER WHAT
YOU LEARNED
FROM TODAY'S
PASSAGE.

REFLECTION
QUESTIONS

1. Why is Paul giving thanks for his brothers and sisters in Thessalonica?

2. What makes the church of the Thessalonians such a good example?

3. What did Paul mean when he said, "We had suffered before and were shamefully entreated at Philippi." (see Acts 16:16-40)

4. What illustrations of sufferings did Paul give to encourage the Thessalonians in their suffering? (14-16). How is this an encouragement?

5. What was Paul's joy and crown of rejoicing? (19-20)

NOTES

WEEK 2

Standing Firm in Faith, Hope & Love

For since we believe that Jesus died and rose again, even so, through Jesus, God will bring with Him those who have fallen asleep.

1 THESSALONIANS 4:14

PRAYER

Prayer focus for this week:
Spend time praying for your country.

MONDAY

TUESDAY

WEDNESDAY

THURSDAY

FRIDAY

CHALLENGE

You can find this listed in our Monday blog post.

MONDAY
Scripture for Week 2

1 Thessalonians 3:1-5
1 Therefore when we could bear it no longer, we were willing to be left behind at Athens alone, 2 and we sent Timothy, our brother and God's coworker in the gospel of Christ, to establish and exhort you in your faith, 3 that no one be moved by these afflictions. For you yourselves know that we are destined for this. 4 For when we were with you, we kept telling you beforehand that we were to suffer affliction, just as it has come to pass, and just as you know. 5 For this reason, when I could bear it no longer, I sent to learn about your faith, for fear that somehow the tempter had tempted you and our labor would be in vain.

MONDAY

READ:
1 Thessalonians 3:1-5

SOAP:
1 Thessalonians 3:2-3

Scripture

WRITE
OUT THE
SCRIPTURE
PASSAGE
FOR THE
DAY.

Observations

WRITE
DOWN 1 OR 2
OBSERVATIONS
FROM THE
PASSAGE.

Applications

WRITE
DOWN 1 OR 2
APPLICATIONS
FROM THE
PASSAGE.

Pray

WRITE OUT
A PRAYER
OVER WHAT
YOU LEARNED
FROM TODAY'S
PASSAGE.

TUESDAY
Scripture for Week 2

1 Thessalonians 3:6-13

6 But now that Timothy has come to us from you, and has brought us the good news of your faith and love and reported that you always remember us kindly and long to see us, as we long to see you— 7 for this reason, brothers, in all our distress and affliction we have been comforted about you through your faith. 8 For now we live, if you are standing fast in the Lord. 9 For what thanksgiving can we return to God for you, for all the joy that we feel for your sake before our God, 10 as we pray most earnestly night and day that we may see you face to face and supply what is lacking in your faith?

11 Now may our God and Father himself, and our Lord Jesus, direct our way to you, 12 and may the Lord make you increase and abound in love for one another and for all, as we do for you, 13 so that he may establish your hearts blameless in holiness before our God and Father, at the coming of our Lord Jesus with all his saints.

TUESDAY

READ:
1 Thessalonians 3:6-13

SOAP:
1 Thessalonians 3:11-13

Scripture

WRITE
OUT THE
SCRIPTURE
PASSAGE
FOR THE
DAY.

Observations

WRITE
DOWN 1 OR 2
OBSERVATIONS
FROM THE
PASSAGE.

Applications

WRITE
DOWN 1 OR 2
APPLICATIONS
FROM THE
PASSAGE.

Pray

WRITE OUT
A PRAYER
OVER WHAT
YOU LEARNED
FROM TODAY'S
PASSAGE.

WEDNESDAY
Scripture for Week 2

1 Thessalonians 4:1-8

1 Finally, then, brothers, we ask and urge you in the Lord Jesus, that as you received from us how you ought to walk and to please God, just as you are doing, that you do so more and more. 2 For you know what instructions we gave you through the Lord Jesus. 3 For this is the will of God, your sanctification: that you abstain from sexual immorality; 4 that each one of you know how to control his own body in holiness and honor, 5 not in the passion of lust like the Gentiles who do not know God; 6 that no one transgress and wrong his brother in this matter, because the Lord is an avenger in all these things, as we told you beforehand and solemnly warned you. 7 For God has not called us for impurity, but in holiness.8 Therefore whoever disregards this, disregards not man but God, who gives his Holy Spirit to you.

WEDNESDAY

READ:
1 Thessalonians 4:1-8

SOAP:
1 Thessalonians 4:3-5

Scripture

WRITE
OUT THE
SCRIPTURE
PASSAGE
FOR THE
DAY.

Observations

WRITE
DOWN 1 OR 2
OBSERVATIONS
FROM THE
PASSAGE.

Applications

WRITE
DOWN 1 OR 2
APPLICATIONS
FROM THE
PASSAGE.

Pray

WRITE OUT
A PRAYER
OVER WHAT
YOU LEARNED
FROM TODAY'S
PASSAGE.

THURSDAY
Scripture for Week 2

1 Thessalonians 4:9-12

9 Now concerning brotherly love you have no need for anyone to write to you, for you yourselves have been taught by God to love one another, 10 for that indeed is what you are doing to all the brothers throughout Macedonia. But we urge you, brothers, to do this more and more, 11 and to aspire to live quietly, and to mind your own affairs, and to work with your hands, as we instructed you, 12 so that you may walk properly before outsiders and be dependent on no one.

THURSDAY

READ:
1 Thessalonians 4:9-12

SOAP:
1 Thessalonians 4:11-12

Scripture

WRITE
OUT THE
SCRIPTURE
PASSAGE
FOR THE
DAY.

Observations

WRITE
DOWN 1 OR 2
OBSERVATIONS
FROM THE
PASSAGE.

Applications

WRITE
DOWN 1 OR 2
APPLICATIONS
FROM THE
PASSAGE.

Pray

WRITE OUT
A PRAYER
OVER WHAT
YOU LEARNED
FROM TODAY'S
PASSAGE.

FRIDAY
Scripture for Week 2

1 Thessalonians 4:13-18
13 But we do not want you to be uninformed, brothers, about those who are asleep, that you may not grieve as others do who have no hope. 14 For since we believe that Jesus died and rose again, even so, through Jesus, God will bring with him those who have fallen asleep. 15 For this we declare to you by a word from the Lord, that we who are alive, who are left until the coming of the Lord, will not precede those who have fallen asleep. 16 For the Lord himself will descend from heaven with a cry of command, with the voice of an archangel, and with the sound of the trumpet of God. And the dead in Christ will rise first. 17 Then we who are alive, who are left, will be caught up together with them in the clouds to meet the Lord in the air, and so we will always be with the Lord. 18 Therefore encourage one another with these words.

FRIDAY

READ:
1 Thessalonians 4:13-18

SOAP:
1 Thessalonians 4:13-14

Scripture

WRITE
OUT THE
SCRIPTURE
PASSAGE
FOR THE
DAY.

Observations

WRITE
DOWN 1 OR 2
OBSERVATIONS
FROM THE
PASSAGE.

Applications

WRITE
DOWN 1 OR 2
APPLICATIONS
FROM THE
PASSAGE.

Pray

WRITE OUT
A PRAYER
OVER WHAT
YOU LEARNED
FROM TODAY'S
PASSAGE.

REFLECTION
QUESTIONS

1. What does Paul mean by being destined for afflictions (vs. 3)?

2. What report did Timothy bring back (vs.6) and what effect did this have on Paul (vs7-9)?

3. What is God's will for you (vs. 3-5)?

4. What does "sanctification" mean and how are we sanctified?

5. According to 1 Thess 4:16-18 how are we to encourage one another? Why is this truth encouraging?

NOTES

WEEK 3

Hold On To The Good

For God has not destined us for wrath,

but to obtain salvation through our

Lord Jesus Christ, who died for us

so that whether we are awake or

asleep we might live with Him.

1 THESSALONIANS. 5:9-10

PRAYER

Prayer focus for this week:
Spend time praying for your friends.

MONDAY

TUESDAY

WEDNESDAY

THURSDAY

FRIDAY

CHALLENGE

You can find this listed in our Monday blog post.

MONDAY
Scripture for Week 3

1 Thessalonians 5:1-3

1 Now concerning the times and the seasons, brothers, you have no need to have anything written to you. 2 For you yourselves are fully aware that the day of the Lord will come like a thief in the night. 3 While people are saying, "There is peace and security," then sudden destruction will come upon them as labor pains come upon a pregnant woman, and they will not escape.

MONDAY

READ:
1 Thessalonians 5:1-3

SOAP:
1 Thessalonians 5:2

Scripture

WRITE
OUT THE
SCRIPTURE
PASSAGE
FOR THE
DAY.

Observations

WRITE
DOWN 1 OR 2
OBSERVATIONS
FROM THE
PASSAGE.

Applications

WRITE
DOWN 1 OR 2
APPLICATIONS
FROM THE
PASSAGE.

Pray

WRITE OUT
A PRAYER
OVER WHAT
YOU LEARNED
FROM TODAY'S
PASSAGE.

TUESDAY
Scripture for Week 3

1 Thessalonians 5:4-8
4 But you are not in darkness, brothers, for that day to surprise
you like a thief. 5 For you are all children of light, children of the
day. We are not of the night or of the darkness.6 So then let us not
sleep, as others do, but let us keep awake and be sober. 7 For those
who sleep, sleep at night, and those who get drunk, are drunk at
night. 8 But since we belong to the day, let us be sober, having put
on the breastplate of faith and love, and for a helmet the hope of
salvation.

TUESDAY

READ:
1 Thessalonians 5:4-8

SOAP:
1 Thessalonians 5:8

Scripture

WRITE
OUT THE
SCRIPTURE
PASSAGE
FOR THE
DAY.

Observations

WRITE
DOWN 1 OR 2
OBSERVATIONS
FROM THE
PASSAGE.

Applications

WRITE
DOWN 1 OR 2
APPLICATIONS
FROM THE
PASSAGE.

Pray

WRITE OUT
A PRAYER
OVER WHAT
YOU LEARNED
FROM TODAY'S
PASSAGE.

WEDNESDAY
Scripture for Week 3

1 Thessalonians 5:9-11
9 For God has not destined us for wrath, but to obtain salvation through our Lord Jesus Christ, 10 who died for us so that whether we are awake or asleep we might live with him. 11 Therefore encourage one another and build one another up, just as you are doing.

WEDNESDAY

READ:
1 Thessalonians 5:9-11

SOAP:
1 Thessalonians 5:9-11

Scripture

WRITE
OUT THE
SCRIPTURE
PASSAGE
FOR THE
DAY.

Observations

WRITE
DOWN 1 OR 2
OBSERVATIONS
FROM THE
PASSAGE.

Applications

WRITE
DOWN 1 OR 2
APPLICATIONS
FROM THE
PASSAGE.

Pray

WRITE OUT
A PRAYER
OVER WHAT
YOU LEARNED
FROM TODAY'S
PASSAGE.

THURSDAY
Scripture for Week 3

1 Thessalonians 5:12-22

12 We ask you, brothers, to respect those who labor among
you and are over you in the Lord and admonish you, 13 and to
esteem them very highly in love because of their work. Be at peace
among yourselves. 14 And we urge you, brothers, admonish the
idle, encourage the fainthearted, help the weak, be patient with
them all. 15 See that no one repays anyone evil for evil, but
always seek to do good to one another and to everyone. 16 Rejoice
always, 17 pray without ceasing, 18 give thanks in all circumstances;
for this is the will of God in Christ Jesus for you. 19 Do not quench
the Spirit. 20 Do not despise prophecies, 21 but test everything;
hold fast what is good. 22 Abstain from every form of evil.

THURSDAY

READ:
1 Thessalonians 5:12-22

SOAP:
1 Thessalonians 5: 14-18

Scripture

WRITE
OUT THE
SCRIPTURE
PASSAGE
FOR THE
DAY.

Observations

WRITE
DOWN 1 OR 2
OBSERVATIONS
FROM THE
PASSAGE.

Applications

WRITE
DOWN 1 OR 2
APPLICATIONS
FROM THE
PASSAGE.

Pray

WRITE OUT
A PRAYER
OVER WHAT
YOU LEARNED
FROM TODAY'S
PASSAGE.

FRIDAY
Scripture for Week 3

1 Thessalonians 5:23-28
23 Now may the God of peace himself sanctify you completely, and may your whole spirit and soul and body be kept blameless at the coming of our Lord Jesus Christ. 24 He who calls you is faithful; he will surely do it.

25 Brothers, pray for us.

26 Greet all the brothers with a holy kiss.

27 I put you under oath before the Lord to have this letter read to all the brothers.

28 The grace of our Lord Jesus Christ be with you.

FRIDAY

READ:
1 Thessalonians 5:23-28

SOAP:
1 Thessalonians 5:24

Scripture

WRITE
OUT THE
SCRIPTURE
PASSAGE
FOR THE
DAY.

Observations

WRITE
DOWN 1 OR 2
OBSERVATIONS
FROM THE
PASSAGE.

Applications

WRITE
DOWN 1 OR 2
APPLICATIONS
FROM THE
PASSAGE.

Pray

WRITE OUT
A PRAYER
OVER WHAT
YOU LEARNED
FROM TODAY'S
PASSAGE.

REFLECTION QUESTIONS

1. How should we think about the return of Christ? How should we prepare ourselves?

2. What is meant by the word sober in verses 6 and 8?

3. Who are the people we are to respect and why?

4. Who are we to be patient with (vs.14)? Why?

5. What does it mean that the Lord is faithful? How does this affect us?

NOTES

WEEK 4

The Hope Of Christ's Return

To this end we always pray for you, that our God may make you worthy of His calling and may fulfill every resolve for good and every work of faith by His power, so that the name of our Lord Jesus may be glorified in you, and you in Him, according to the grace of our God and the Lord Jesus Christ.

2 THESSALONIANS. 1:11-12

PRAYER

Prayer focus for this week:
Spend time praying for your church.

MONDAY

TUESDAY

WEDNESDAY

THURSDAY

FRIDAY

CHALLENGE

You can find this listed in our Monday blog post.

MONDAY
Scripture for Week 4

2 Thessalonians 1:1-2
1 Paul, Silvanus, and Timothy,

To the church of the Thessalonians in God our Father and the Lord Jesus Christ:

2 Grace to you and peace from God our Father and the Lord Jesus Christ.

MONDAY

READ:
2 Thessalonians 1:1-2

SOAP:
2 Thessalonians 1:2

Scripture

WRITE
OUT THE
SCRIPTURE
PASSAGE
FOR THE
DAY.

Observations

WRITE
DOWN 1 OR 2
OBSERVATIONS
FROM THE
PASSAGE.

Applications

WRITE
DOWN 1 OR 2
APPLICATIONS
FROM THE
PASSAGE.

Pray

WRITE OUT
A PRAYER
OVER WHAT
YOU LEARNED
FROM TODAY'S
PASSAGE.

TUESDAY
Scripture for Week 4

2 Thessalonians 1:3-4
3 We ought always to give thanks to God for you, brothers, as is right, because your faith is growing abundantly, and the love of every one of you for one another is increasing. 4 Therefore we ourselves boast about you in the churches of God for your steadfastness and faith in all your persecutions and in the afflictions that you are enduring.

TUESDAY

READ:
2 Thessalonians 1:3-4

SOAP:
2 Thessalonians 1:3-4

Scripture

WRITE
OUT THE
SCRIPTURE
PASSAGE
FOR THE
DAY.

Observations

WRITE
DOWN 1 OR 2
OBSERVATIONS
FROM THE
PASSAGE.

Applications

WRITE
DOWN 1 OR 2
APPLICATIONS
FROM THE
PASSAGE.

Pray

WRITE OUT
A PRAYER
OVER WHAT
YOU LEARNED
FROM TODAY'S
PASSAGE.

WEDNESDAY
Scripture for Week 4

2 Thessalonians 1:5-8
5 This is evidence of the righteous judgment of God, that you may
be considered worthy of the kingdom of God, for which you are
also suffering— 6 since indeed God considers it just to repay with
affliction those who afflict you, 7 and to grant relief to you who
are afflicted as well as to us, when the Lord Jesus is revealed from
heaven with his mighty angels 8 in flaming fire, inflicting vengeance
on those who do not know God and on those who do not obey the
gospel of our Lord Jesus.

WEDNESDAY

READ:
READ:
2 Thessalonians 1:5-8

SOAP:
2 Thessalonians 1:6-8

Scripture

WRITE
OUT THE
SCRIPTURE
PASSAGE
FOR THE
DAY.

Observations

WRITE
DOWN 1 OR 2
OBSERVATIONS
FROM THE
PASSAGE.

Applications

WRITE
DOWN 1 OR 2
APPLICATIONS
FROM THE
PASSAGE.

Pray

WRITE OUT
A PRAYER
OVER WHAT
YOU LEARNED
FROM TODAY'S
PASSAGE.

THURSDAY
Scripture for Week 4

2 Thessalonians 1:9-10
9 They will suffer the punishment of eternal destruction, away
from the presence of the Lord and from the glory of his
might, 10 when he comes on that day to be glorified in his saints,
and to be marveled at among all who have believed, because
our testimony to you was believed.

THURSDAY

READ:
2 Thessalonians 1:9-10

SOAP:
2 Thessalonians 1:10

Scripture

WRITE
OUT THE
SCRIPTURE
PASSAGE
FOR THE
DAY.

Observations

WRITE
DOWN 1 OR 2
OBSERVATIONS
FROM THE
PASSAGE.

Applications

WRITE
DOWN 1 OR 2
APPLICATIONS
FROM THE
PASSAGE.

Pray

WRITE OUT
A PRAYER
OVER WHAT
YOU LEARNED
FROM TODAY'S
PASSAGE.

FRIDAY
Scripture for Week 4

2 Thessalonians 1:11-12
11 To this end we always pray for you, that our God may make you worthy of his calling and may fulfill every resolve for good and every work of faith by his power, 12 so that the name of our Lord Jesus may be glorified in you, and you in him, according to the grace of our God and the Lord Jesus Christ.

FRIDAY

READ:
2 Thessalonians 1:11-12

SOAP:
2 Thessalonians 1:11

Scripture

WRITE
OUT THE
SCRIPTURE
PASSAGE
FOR THE
DAY.

Observations

WRITE
DOWN 1 OR 2
OBSERVATIONS
FROM THE
PASSAGE.

Applications

WRITE DOWN 1 OR 2 APPLICATIONS FROM THE PASSAGE.

Pray

WRITE OUT A PRAYER OVER WHAT YOU LEARNED FROM TODAY'S PASSAGE.

REFLECTION
QUESTIONS

1. For what three things did Paul commend the Thessalonian church? (vs3-
   4) Do you see any of these traits in your life?

2. Faith and love are the distinguishing marks of a healthy church. How can
   we grow in love and faith?

3. What will happen to those who do not know God and don't obey the
   gospel? (vs. 8-9)

4. What is the calling (vs. 11) that we are to be worthy of? How are do we
   become worthy of God's calling?

5. What was Paul's prayer for the Thessalonians? (11-12)

NOTES

WEEK 5

Our Good Hope

But we ought always to give thanks to God for you, brothers beloved by the Lord, because God chose you as the firstfruits to be saved, through sanctification by the Spirit and belief in the truth.

2 THESSALONIANS. 2:13

PRAYER

Prayer focus for this week:
Spend time praying for missionaries.

MONDAY

TUESDAY

WEDNESDAY

THURSDAY

FRIDAY

CHALLENGE

You can find this listed in our Monday blog post.

MONDAY

Scripture for Week 5

2 Thessalonians 2:1-2

1 Now concerning the coming of our Lord Jesus Christ and
our being gathered together to him, we ask you, brothers, 2 not to
be quickly shaken in mind or alarmed, either by a spirit or a spoken
word, or a letter seeming to be from us, to the effect that the day of
the Lord has come.

MONDAY

READ:
2 Thessalonians 2:1-2

SOAP:
2 Thessalonians 2:2

Scripture

WRITE
OUT THE
SCRIPTURE
PASSAGE
FOR THE
DAY.

Observations

WRITE
DOWN 1 OR 2
OBSERVATIONS
FROM THE
PASSAGE.

Applications

WRITE
DOWN 1 OR 2
APPLICATIONS
FROM THE
PASSAGE.

Pray

WRITE OUT
A PRAYER
OVER WHAT
YOU LEARNED
FROM TODAY'S
PASSAGE.

TUESDAY
Scripture for Week 5

2 Thessalonians 2:3-4

3 Let no one deceive you in any way. For that day will not come, unless the rebellion comes first, and the man of lawlessness is revealed, the son of destruction, 4 who opposes and exalts himself against every so-called god or object of worship, so that he takes his seat in the temple of God, proclaiming himself to be God.

TUESDAY

READ:
2 Thessalonians 2:3-4

SOAP:
2 Thessalonians 2:3

Scripture

WRITE
OUT THE
SCRIPTURE
PASSAGE
FOR THE
DAY.

Observations

WRITE
DOWN 1 OR 2
OBSERVATIONS
FROM THE
PASSAGE.

Applications

WRITE
DOWN 1 OR 2
APPLICATIONS
FROM THE
PASSAGE.

Pray

WRITE OUT
A PRAYER
OVER WHAT
YOU LEARNED
FROM TODAY'S
PASSAGE.

WEDNESDAY
Scripture for Week 5

2 Thessalonians 2:5-8
5 Do you not remember that when I was still with you I told you these things? 6 And you know what is restraining him now so that he may be revealed in his time. 7 For the mystery of lawlessness is already at work. Only he who now restrains it will do so until he is out of the way. 8 And then the lawless one will be revealed, whom the Lord Jesus will kill with the breath of his mouth and bring to nothing by the appearance of his coming.

WEDNESDAY

READ:
2 Thessalonians 2:5-8

SOAP:
2 Thessalonians 2:7

Scripture

WRITE
OUT THE
SCRIPTURE
PASSAGE
FOR THE
DAY.

Observations

WRITE
DOWN 1 OR 2
OBSERVATIONS
FROM THE
PASSAGE.

Applications

WRITE
DOWN 1 OR 2
APPLICATIONS
FROM THE
PASSAGE.

Pray

WRITE OUT
A PRAYER
OVER WHAT
YOU LEARNED
FROM TODAY'S
PASSAGE.

THURSDAY
Scripture for Week 5

2 Thessalonians 2:9-12

9 The coming of the lawless one is by the activity of Satan with all power and false signs and wonders, 10 and with all wicked deception for those who are perishing, because they refused to love the truth and so be saved.

11 Therefore God sends them a strong delusion, so that they may believe what is false, 12 in order that all may be condemned who did not believe the truth but had pleasure in unrighteousness.

THURSDAY

READ:
2 Thessalonians 2:9-12

SOAP:
2 Thessalonians 2:10

Scripture

WRITE
OUT THE
SCRIPTURE
PASSAGE
FOR THE
DAY.

Observations

WRITE
DOWN 1 OR 2
OBSERVATIONS
FROM THE
PASSAGE.

Applications

WRITE
DOWN 1 OR 2
APPLICATIONS
FROM THE
PASSAGE.

Pray

WRITE OUT
A PRAYER
OVER WHAT
YOU LEARNED
FROM TODAY'S
PASSAGE.

FRIDAY
Scripture for Week 5

2 Thessalonians 2:13-17

13 But we ought always to give thanks to God for you, brothers beloved by the Lord, because God chose you as the firstfruits to be saved, through sanctification by the Spirit and belief in the truth. 14 To this he called you through our gospel, so that you may obtain the glory of our Lord Jesus Christ. 15 So then, brothers, stand firm and hold to the traditions that you were taught by us, either by our spoken word or by our letter.

16 Now may our Lord Jesus Christ himself, and God our Father, who loved us and gave us eternal comfort and good hope through grace, 17 comfort your hearts and establish them in every good work and word.

FRIDAY

READ:
2 Thessalonians 2:13-17

SOAP:
2 Thessalonians 2:13

Scripture

WRITE
OUT THE
SCRIPTURE
PASSAGE
FOR THE
DAY.

Observations

WRITE
DOWN 1 OR 2
OBSERVATIONS
FROM THE
PASSAGE.

Applications

WRITE
DOWN 1 OR 2
APPLICATIONS
FROM THE
PASSAGE.

Pray

WRITE OUT
A PRAYER
OVER WHAT
YOU LEARNED
FROM TODAY'S
PASSAGE.

REFLECTION QUESTIONS

1. What three things did Paul say the Thessalonians should not be shaken in mind or troubled by? (vs2)

2. What two things must take place before the day of Christ (Day of the Lord) can come? (vs3)

3. What will the "man of lawlessness" be like? (vs.3-4)

4. Why is it important that we have a strong faith?

5. In what ways does Christ comfort us?

NOTES

WEEK 6

Praying & Working

---

*As for you, brothers,
do not grow weary in doing good.*

2 THESSALONIANS. 3:13

PRAYER

WRITE DOWN YOUR PRAYER REQUESTS
AND PRAISES FOR EACH DAY.

Prayer focus for this week:
Spend time praying for you.

MONDAY

TUESDAY

WEDNESDAY

THURSDAY

FRIDAY

CHALLENGE

You can find this listed in our Monday blog post.

MONDAY

Scripture for Week 6

2 Thessalonians 3:1-5

1 Finally, brothers, pray for us, that the word of the Lord may speed ahead and be honored, as happened among you, 2 and that we may be delivered from wicked and evil men. For not all have faith. 3 But the Lord is faithful. He will establish you and guard you against the evil one. 4 And we have confidence in the Lord about you, that you are doing and will do the things that we command. 5 May the Lord direct your hearts to the love of God and to the steadfastness of Christ.

MONDAY

READ:
2 Thessalonians 3:1-5

SOAP:
2 Thessalonians 3:3

Scripture

WRITE
OUT THE
SCRIPTURE
PASSAGE
FOR THE
DAY.

Observations

WRITE
DOWN 1 OR 2
OBSERVATIONS
FROM THE
PASSAGE.

Applications

WRITE
DOWN 1 OR 2
APPLICATIONS
FROM THE
PASSAGE.

Pray

WRITE OUT
A PRAYER
OVER WHAT
YOU LEARNED
FROM TODAY'S
PASSAGE.

TUESDAY
Scripture for Week 6

2 Thessalonians 3:6-9

6 Now we command you, brothers, in the name of our Lord Jesus Christ, that you keep away from any brother who is walking in idleness and not in accord with the tradition that you received from us. 7 For you yourselves know how you ought to imitate us, because we were not idle when we were with you, 8 nor did we eat anyone's bread without paying for it, but with toil and labor we worked night and day, that we might not be a burden to any of you. 9 It was not because we do not have that right, but to give you in ourselves an example to imitate.

TUESDAY

READ:
2 Thessalonians 3:6-9

SOAP:
2 Thessalonians 3:9

Scripture

WRITE
OUT THE
SCRIPTURE
PASSAGE
FOR THE
DAY.

Observations

WRITE
DOWN 1 OR 2
OBSERVATIONS
FROM THE
PASSAGE.

Applications

WRITE
DOWN 1 OR 2
APPLICATIONS
FROM THE
PASSAGE.

Pray

WRITE OUT
A PRAYER
OVER WHAT
YOU LEARNED
FROM TODAY'S
PASSAGE.

WEDNESDAY
Scripture for Week 6

2 Thessalonians 3:10-12
10 For even when we were with you, we would give you this command: If anyone is not willing to work, let him not eat. 11 For we hear that some among you walk in idleness, not busy at work, but busybodies. 12 Now such persons we command and encourage in the Lord Jesus Christ to do their work quietly and to earn their own living.

WEDNESDAY

READ:
2 Thessalonians 3:10-12

SOAP:
2 Thessalonians 3:10

Scripture

WRITE
OUT THE
SCRIPTURE
PASSAGE
FOR THE
DAY.

Observations

WRITE
DOWN 1 OR 2
OBSERVATIONS
FROM THE
PASSAGE.

Applications

WRITE
DOWN 1 OR 2
APPLICATIONS
FROM THE
PASSAGE.

Pray

WRITE OUT
A PRAYER
OVER WHAT
YOU LEARNED
FROM TODAY'S
PASSAGE.

THURSDAY
Scripture for Week 6

2 Thessalonians 3:13-15
13 As for you, brothers, do not grow weary in doing good. 14 If anyone does not obey what we say in this letter, take note of that person, and have nothing to do with him, that he may be ashamed. 15 Do not regard him as an enemy, but warn him as a brother.

THURSDAY

READ:
2 Thessalonians 3:13-15

SOAP:
2 Thessalonians 3:13

Scripture

WRITE
OUT THE
SCRIPTURE
PASSAGE
FOR THE
DAY.

Observations

WRITE
DOWN 1 OR 2
OBSERVATIONS
FROM THE
PASSAGE.

Applications

WRITE
DOWN 1 OR 2
APPLICATIONS
FROM THE
PASSAGE.

Pray

WRITE OUT
A PRAYER
OVER WHAT
YOU LEARNED
FROM TODAY'S
PASSAGE.

FRIDAY

Scripture for Week 6

2 Thessalonians 3:16-18

16 Now may the Lord of peace himself give you peace at all times in every way. The Lord be with you all.

17 I, Paul, write this greeting with my own hand. This is the sign of genuineness in every letter of mine; it is the way I write. 18 The grace of our Lord Jesus Christ be with you all.

FRIDAY

READ:
2 Thessalonians 3:16-18

SOAP:
2 Thessalonians 3:16

Scripture

WRITE
OUT THE
SCRIPTURE
PASSAGE
FOR THE
DAY.

Observations

WRITE
DOWN 1 OR 2
OBSERVATIONS
FROM THE
PASSAGE.

Applications

WRITE
DOWN 1 OR 2
APPLICATIONS
FROM THE
PASSAGE.

Pray

WRITE OUT
A PRAYER
OVER WHAT
YOU LEARNED
FROM TODAY'S
PASSAGE.

REFLECTION QUESTIONS

1. What did Paul want the Thessalonians to pray about? (1-2)

2. Why is Paul so hard on people who don't work?

3. Why is having a good work ethic so important?

4. What can people turn into who don't work? (10-11)

5. How does Galatians 6:9 compare to verse 13?

NOTES

KNOW THESE TRUTHS
from God's Word

God loves you.
Even when you're feeling unworthy and like the world is stacked against you, God loves you - yes, you - and He has created you for great purpose.

God's Word says, "God so loved the world that He gave His one and only Son, Jesus, that whoever believes in Him shall not perish, but have eternal life" (John 3:16).

Our sin separates us from God.
We are all sinners by nature and by choice, and because of this we are separated from God, who is holy.

God's Word says, "All have sinned and fall short of the glory of God" (Romans 3:23).

Jesus died so that you might have life.
The consequence of sin is death, but your story doesn't have to end there! God's free gift of salvation is available to us because Jesus took the penalty for our sin when He died on the cross.

God's Word says, "For the wages of sin is death, but the free gift of God is eternal life in Christ Jesus our Lord" (Romans 6:23); "God demonstrates His own love toward us, in that while we were yet sinners, Christ died for us" (Romans 5:8).

Jesus lives!
Death could not hold Him, and three days after His body was placed in the tomb Jesus rose again, defeating sin and death forever! He lives today in heaven and is preparing a place in eternity for all who believe in Him.

God's Word says, "In my Father's house are many rooms. If it were not so, would I have told you that I go to prepare a place for you? And if I go and prepare a place for you, I will come again and will take you to myself, that where I am you may be also" (John 14:2-3).

Yes, you can KNOW that you are forgiven.
Accept Jesus as the only way to salvation...

Accepting Jesus as your Savior is not about what you can do, but rather about having faith in what Jesus has already done. It takes recognizing that you are a sinner, believing that Jesus died for your sins, and asking for forgiveness by placing your full trust in Jesus's work on the cross on your behalf.

God's Word says, "If you confess with your mouth that Jesus is Lord and believe in your heart that God raised him from the dead, you will be saved. For with the heart one believes and is justified, and with the mouth one confesses and is saved" (Romans 10:9-10).

Practically, what does that look like?
With a sincere heart, you can pray a simple prayer like this:

God,
I know that I am a sinner.
I don't want to live another day without embracing
the love and forgiveness that You have for me.
I ask for Your forgiveness.
I believe that You died for my sins and rose from the dead.
I surrender all that I am and ask You to be Lord of my life.
Help me to turn from my sin and follow You.
Teach me what it means to walk in freedom as I live under Your grace,
and help me to grow in Your ways as I seek to know You more.
Amen.

If you just prayed this prayer (or something similar in your own words), would you email us at info@lovegodgreatly.com?

We'd love to help get you started on this exciting journey as a child of God!

WELCOME FRIEND

We're so glad you're here

Love God Greatly exists to inspire, encourage, and equip women all over the world to make God's Word a priority in their lives.

INSPIRE
women to make God's Word a priority in their daily lives through our Bible study resources.

ENCOURAGE
women in their daily walks with God through online community and personal accountability.

EQUIP
women to grow in their faith, so that they can effectively reach others for Christ.

Love God Greatly consists of a beautiful community of women who use a variety of technology platforms to keep each other accountable in God's Word.

We start with a simple Bible reading plan, but it doesn't stop there.

Some gather in homes and churches locally, while others connect online with women across the globe. Whatever the method, we lovingly lock arms and unite for this purpose...to Love God Greatly with our lives.

At Love God Greatly, you'll find real, authentic women. Women who are imperfect, yet forgiven. Women who desire less of us, and a whole lot more of Jesus. Women who long to know God through his Word, because we know that Truth transforms and sets us free. Women who are better together, saturated in God's Word and in community with one another.

Love God Greatly is a 501 (C) (3) non-profit organization. Funding for Love God Greatly comes through donations and proceeds from our online Bible study journals and books. LGG is committed to providing quality Bible study materials and believes finances should never get in the way of a woman being able to participate in one of our studies. All journals and translated journals are available to download for free from LoveGodGreatly.com for those who cannot afford to purchase them. Our journals and books are also available for sale on Amazon. Search for "Love God Greatly" to see all of our Bible study journals and books. 100% of proceeds go directly back into supporting Love God Greatly and helping us inspire, encourage and equip women all over the world with God's Word.

THANK YOU for partnering with us!

WHAT WE OFFER:

18 + Translations | Bible Reading Plans | Online Bible Study
Love God Greatly App | 80 + Countries Served
Bible Study Journals & Books | Community Groups

EACH LGG STUDY INCLUDES:

Three Devotional Corresponding Blog Posts
Memory Verses | Weekly Challenge | Weekly Reading Plan
Reflection Questions And More!

OTHER LOVE GOD GREATLY STUDIES INCLUDE:

David | Ecclesiastes | Growing Through Prayer | Names Of God
Galatians | Psalm 119 | 1st & 2nd Peter | Made For Community | Esther
The Road To Christmas | The Source Of Gratitude | You Are Loved

Visit us online at
LOVEGODGREATLY.COM

Made in the USA
Lexington, KY
14 April 2018